My Brother Is Autistic

Text: *Jennifer Moore-Mallinos*

Illustrations: *Marta Fàbrega*

BARRON'S

Do you have any brothers or sisters?
I do! I have one brother; his name is Billy
and he has autism. Billy and I often have
a lot of fun together. Most of the time
we get along, but I don't like it when he
freaks out, especially in front of my friends
or the other kids at school.

Like yesterday at school. We were sitting in the cafeteria eating lunch together, and Billy had just finished lining his cookies up in a straight line, like he always does before he eats them, and one of the kids at the table asked Billy if he could have a cookie. Billy ignored the boy and kept admiring his row of cookies, so the boy asked again. This time Billy repeated the boy's question, and the boy thought Billy was making fun of him so he leaned over and grabbed one of Billy's cookies.

And that's when it happened!

Billy got mad! He squinted his eyes, started flapping his hands in the air, and squealed really loud. Then he stood up, flipped over his lunch tray, and kept flapping his arms. Billy's shriek was so loud that everybody had to cover their ears. And everybody knew that he was my brother! I was so embarrassed that, instead of trying to calm him down, I ran out of the cafeteria as fast as I could and left Billy with all that mess he had made.

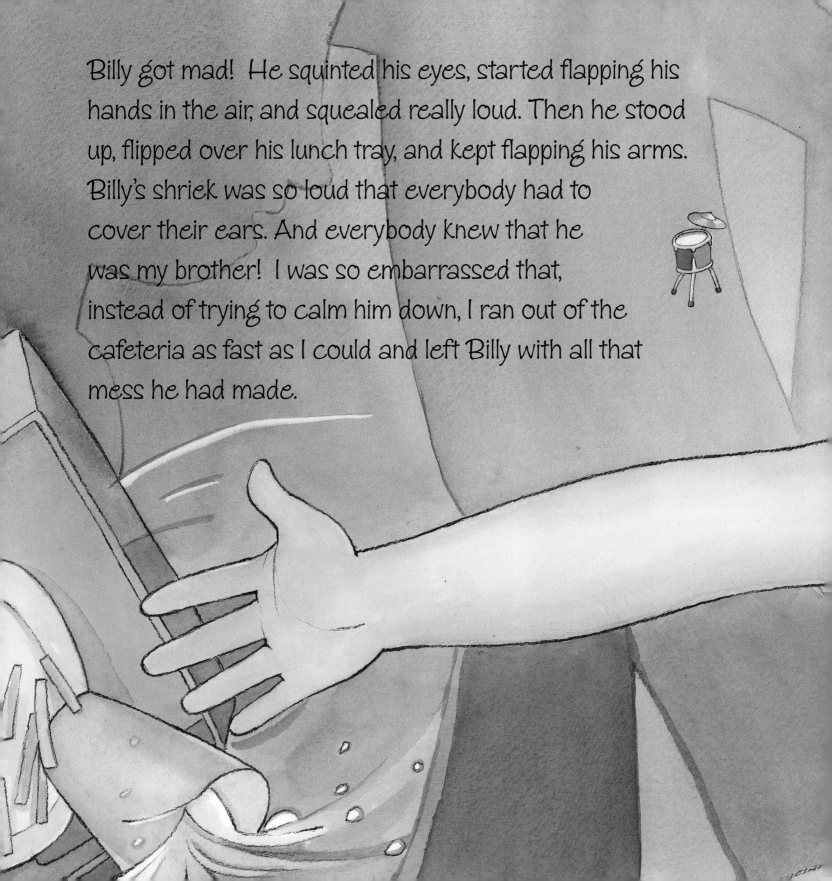

I kept running until I was stopped in the hall by my teacher, Mrs. Smitty. I told Mrs. Smitty what had happened and how everybody, especially the kids in my class, were staring and pointing at Billy and how some were even laughing at him!

I knew that the kid wasn't trying to be mean when he took Billy's cookie; he just didn't understand that Billy likes things to be the same, and that includes the way he lines his cookies in a row before he eats them. Whenever things change too quickly Billy will do certain things over and over again, like flapping his arms or rocking back and forth, to help him feel better. Maybe if the kid knew more about autism he wouldn't have taken one of Billy's cookies . . .

he would have known how important it is for Billy to do things always the same way. I told my teacher that I wished more kids understood autism, because if they did, then maybe they'd give kids like Billy a chance!

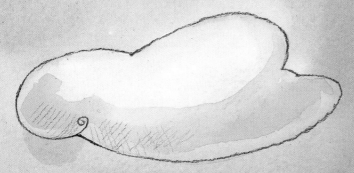

Mrs. Smitty told me that there are many scientists trying to find out what causes autism, but nobody knows for sure yet. Some people think that autism may run in families, while others believe that kids with autism have special allergies and sensitivities that make them think and behave differently. The brains of autistic children do work differently from other people's brains. Autism can't be cured, and that's why everybody in the family has to learn to share the problem. Mrs. Smitty said that teasing and making fun of Billy was bad, and that we should help the other kids understand. Then Mrs. Smitty said that she had an idea, and she hurried down to her classroom.

When the bell rang and it was time
to go back to class, I got a little
scared about seeing the other kids;
I didn't want them to start
making jokes about Billy
like they did before.
But when I walked into my
class, Mrs. Smitty and a few of the
other kids were busy taping a whole
bunch of pictures to the board, so
nobody noticed me when I came
in and sat down.

All of the pictures were of different people, young and old, doing different things. One picture was of a young man playing the piano and another was of a girl playing tennis. There was even a picture of an old man painting a portrait of a beautiful lady. The picture I liked the best was of a boy named Jason McElwain, who made the winning basket for our basketball team. He looked so happy! All of these people were doing things they liked, and they were good at doing them, and all of these people had autism.

At first I couldn't figure out what all these pictures of people I didn't even know had to do with Billy, but when Mrs. Smitty asked the class what each person on the board and one in every 150 American kids had in common, I figured it out! All these people, who were so good at doing different things, had autism, just like Billy! Not everybody with autism will become famous and, just like everybody else, some will be able to do more things than others. And that's okay because that's what makes us all special!

20-21

Wow! It was hard to believe it, but it was true:
Even though all these people had autism, they
all found something that they were really good at doing.
Billy's really good at playing the drums, so maybe when
he grows up he'll play in a band and, being his brother,
he'll give me front-row tickets to watch him play!
Now, that would be cool!

Mrs. Smitty talked a lot about what it meant to have autism. She said that some autistic kids might have trouble doing what their teacher or parents ask them to do and other kids might get frustrated and upset really quick when something changes, just like Billy's row of cookies. Most kids with autism like to do things alone and, because they have trouble starting a conversation with others, it's not always easy for them to make friends. Others have trouble learning things like reading and writing and math. Billy needs some extra help, so he has a special teacher who stays with him in class and helps him when he needs it.

When the class was over and the kids all left, I thanked Mrs. Smitty for what she had done. Not only did she make it clear that Billy had the right to be himself, a kid with autism, but she also made it okay for me to be his brother without feeling embarrassed. I'll never leave Billy alone again. And next time Billy gets mad or is chattering to himself, I hope the other kids will remember that Billy has autism and that's okay!

 Going back home with Billy, I realized that now I saw him not only for who he is, but for who he could become. I told Billy that I was sorry for leaving him all alone in the cafeteria and I promised that no matter what, I would never do that again. Billy smiled, touched my shoulder, and said "you're IT" and then ran away. Just like always, I counted to ten before I started chasing him and, just like always, Billy ran as fast as he could all the way home!

Note to parents

The purpose of this book is to acknowledge the prevalence of autism among children and to recognize some of the realities children with autism and their families—their siblings in particular—may experience. This book allows us the opportunity to consider some of the challenges a sibling of an autistic child may experience on a regular basis and among his peers.

It is hoped that this book will promote a better understanding and acceptance of children who have been diagnosed with autism and also of the difficulties their siblings must face.

Did you know that according to the Autism Society of America, 1 in every 150 children will be born with autism? And many of these children with autism have brothers and sisters.

Many siblings of children with autism will often share common concerns and similar sources of stress, including the fear of becoming the target of teasing and ridicule among their peers, and experiencing feelings of embarrassment, frustration, and even anger toward the child's autistic behaviors. Some children may also feel some level of resentment toward their parents and/or teachers, believing that they are not receiving the same amount of attention as their sibling with autism and therefore are not being treated fairly.

Autism is considered a spectrum disorder characterized by a set of behaviors exhibited along a continuum, ranging from mild to quite severe. Although an individual may display a combination of behavioral traits that fall within a specific range from mild to severe, autism is unique to one's personality.

According to the Autism Society of America, children who are diagnosed at an early age are able to benefit from specialized programs and education sooner and therefore seem to have dramatically better outcomes overall.

Behaviors that are characteristic of autism are usually first detected through the parents' observations of their child's everyday behavior, including his or her ability to communicate and socialize with others. Distinguishing autistic traits may not become apparent until the child's early childhood years, between the ages of 2 and 6. Each new developmental stage offers new opportunities to observe autistic behaviors, and to note the child's level of success when he or she copes with them.

According to the Autism Society of America, a person with autism may display the following characteristics:

- aggressive/self–injurious behavior
- resistance to change
- difficulty in expressing needs
- repetition of words or phrases
- tantrums
- difficulty in socializing with others
- nonresponsiveness to verbal cues (appears not to hear, despite testing within normal range in hearing tests)
- prefers being alone
- little or no eye contact
- eagerness to spin objects, "odd" play
- sensitiveness to loud noises

Although siblings of autistic children seem to cope well overall, there are some steps that parents can take to help reduce conflicts in everyday life:

- Giving children (siblings) the information they need to understand autism is always a good idea. The information you provide should take into account your children's age and level of understanding. Explaining autism to children should start early and be done often. As your children mature, so will the information you provide them.
- Some children may have a difficult time forming a relationship with their sibling with autism. Their attempts to engage them will not always be successful, leaving them feeling rejected and discouraged from trying again. Parents can help their children by teaching them simple skills that are conducive to positive interaction with their autistic brother or sister; for example, making sure that the autistic sibling is paying attention, giving him or her simple instructions, and providing ongoing praise during play.
- Provide one-on-one time with the other children in the family. Make it clear that they are as important and loved as the autistic sibling. All children want to feel special and to feel that things around them are fair or equal, especially at home!

Growing up in a family with a child who has autism can be difficult at times, but most family members seem to cope well. One advantage in this situation is the fact that siblings will learn to deal with specific issues sooner in life than others, and they will discover that the love, patience, and sense of humor they have learned are vital life skills that they can use for the rest of their lives.

MY BROTHER IS AUTISTIC

First edition for the United States
and Canada published in 2008 by
Barron's Educational Series, Inc.
© Copyright 2008 by Gemser Publications, S.L.
C/Castell, 38; Teià (08329), Barcelona, Spain
(World Rights)
Author: Jennifer Moore-Mallinos
Illustrator: Marta Fàbrega

All inquiries should be addressed to:
Barron's Educational Series, Inc.
250 Wireless Boulevard
Hauppauge, NY 11788
www.barronseduc.com

ISBN-13: 978-0-7641-4044-0
ISBN-10: 0-7641-4044-2
Library of Congress Control Number: 2007941409

Printed in China
9 8 7 6 5 4 3 2 1